REBECCA WEST: A Life

ALSO BY VICTORIA GLENDINNING

Vita: The Life of V. Sackville-West
(1983)

Edith Sitwell: A Unicorn Among Lions
(1981)

Elizabeth Bowen: Portrait of a Writer
(1978)

A Suppressed Cry
(1969)

REBECCA WEST

A Life

VICTORIA GLENDINNING

FAWCETT COLUMBINE • NEW YORK

A Fawcett Columbine Book
Published by Ballantine Books
Copyright © 1987 by Victoria Glendinning

Originally published in Great Britain by Weidenfeld & Nicolson, London.

Grateful acknowledgment is made to the following libraries for permission to reprint
material from their collections: Harry Ransom Humanities Research Center, The University of Texas at Austin; Beinecke Rare Book and Manuscript Library, Yale University; Dorothy Thompson Collection, George Arents Research Library for Special
Collections, Syracuse University; Lilly Library, Indiana University; and the Henry W.
and Albert A. Berg Collection, The New York Public Library, Astor, Lenox and Tilden
Foundations.

Excerpts from unpublished letters of H. G. Wells reprinted by permission of AP Watt
on behalf of the Literary Executors of the Estate of H. G. Wells.

Grateful acknowledgment is made to the following for permission to reprint previously
published material: *Harcourt Brace Jovanovich, Inc.*: Excerpts from *The Letters of Virginia
Woolf,* Volumes 2, 3, 5, and 6, edited by Nigel Nicolson. Excerpts from *The Diary of
Virginia Woolf,* Volume IV, edited by Anne Oliver Bell. Reprinted by permission of the publisher.

Little Brown and Company: Excerpts from *H. G. Wells in Love,* edited by G. P. Wells.
Copyright © 1984 by the Executors of the Estate of H. G. Wells. Reprinted by permission of Little Brown and Company.

AP Watt Ltd.: Excerpts from *H. G. Wells and Rebecca West,* edited by Gordon N. Ray.
Reprinted by permission of AP Watt on behalf of the Literary Executors
of the Estate of H. G. Wells.

Library of Congress Catalog Card Number: 87-91900

ISBN: 0-449-90320-6

This edition published by arrangement with Alfred A. Knopf, Inc.

Cover design by Richard Aquan
Photo: Weidenfeld & Nicolson Ltd.

Manufactured in the United States of America

First Ballantine Books Edition: October 1988

10 9 8 7 6 5 4 3 2 1

PART ONE

Cissie

1

In the year 1900 the three Fairfield girls were fifteen, thirteen, and seven. Their names were Letitia, Winifred, and Cicely Isabel, known in the family as Lettie, Winnie, and Cissie. They lived with their parents at 9 Hermitage Road, Richmond-on-Thames, an unremarkable house in the ancient town on the south-western edge of London. All three children were intelligent and good-looking. They were attending Richmond Church of England High School; in a group photograph, Cissie is sitting in a white smock with the smallest pupils in the front row. Lettie, who loved and indulged this turbulent youngest sister, identified the small boy beside Cissie in a note on the back as "Edward, her adoring boy friend." Cissie did not enjoy school. She was outraged when required to fall on her knees with the headmistress and pray, as a consequence of her misdemeanours, and she herself caused outrage by her irreverent reaction to this performance. Cissie is the future Rebecca West.

The Fairfield family had plenty of books, music, and animated talk about ideas, the arts, politics, and current events. What they did not have was money, and the possibility of catastrophe lay just below the surface. The girls felt different from other children. People who were as poor as their parents were not usually so fiercely articulate and intellectual, while people with their interests and aspirations mostly had newer clothes and better houses. They were not well established in Richmond; their parents' married life had been nomadic. Papa, who was a journalist, had not been lucky.

The girls were precocious readers, steeped from an early age in literature and history: *The Three Musketeers* and *The Count of Monte Cristo* "taught one in the nursery what romance was." So did their own family history. Cissie was to describe herself in print as "an Englishwoman," but she was Scots-Irish, a Celt. Their father was Anglo-Irish, from a family that had served the British Army in Ireland since the seventeenth century. Their mother was Scottish, and the pair had met and married in

Australia, where the two elder girls had been born. The youngest by more than five years, Cissie may have represented a final bid on her parents' part to make their marriage work. After her birth, they ceased to share a bedroom, and in 1901, the year Queen Victoria died, the girls' father left home.

2

Charles Fairfield was a romantic figure to his daughters. With his tales of past glories he filled their heads with pride of family and the sense of a "real life" that should properly be theirs. They never relinquished this image of paradise lost. As he walked with them in Richmond Park, he told them about long-ago Fairfields and his own childhood in Ireland, interspersing his stories with instruction on gentlemanly topics such as the points of a horse.

The early history of the Fairfields is hazy. In 1948 Cissie met one Wynne Fairfield, who had been looking it all up: "Apparently we lived for something like three hundred years on the product of the thrift and intelligence of a Southwark butcher called John Fairfield who died in 1498, having bought land which was finally surrounded by London." Papa's father, Charles George Fairfield, had, like his grandfather, been a military man, and came from County Longford in Ireland. There was a family legend about Charles George's parentage; it was said that he was the natural son of a member of the royal house of Hanover, and that a personal allowance from the royal family accounted for his relative prosperity. Charles George was said, in his turn, to have been the natural father of the famous journalist George Augustus Sala, whose mother was an opera singer—thus providing Papa and his brothers with a distinguished if unacknowledged half-brother. Neither story is verifiable.

Charles George Fairfield married Frances Crosbie, from a well-established County Kerry family. She died, and in 1833 he married Arabella Rowan, the grandmother of the three girls walking with their father in Richmond Park. They heard how their father and his three brothers had ridden and swum and fished in the Kerry countryside. They heard about the sociable "Kerry cousinhood"—the network of Protestant gentry, Fairfields, Rowans, Crosbies, Blennerhassetts, Dennys, some of them powers in the land and some of them rough and wild. The girls' grandfather had bred greyhounds, and became High Sheriff of Kerry. A Denny and a Crosbie had fought a famous duel in the eighteenth century; a Denny ancestor had been cousin to Sir Walter Raleigh; a connection with the Sackvilles gave them descent from an aunt of Anne Boleyn.

Charles Fairfield bequeathed to his daughters an addiction to exotic genealogy. In her old age, Cissie would trace their exiguous connections with noble families all over the British Isles. Lettie, who became a Roman Catholic, was to work out their lines of descent from St. Margaret of Scotland, St. Louis of France, two Russian saints, and a Spanish one. These pedigrees gave them a sense of continuity; the Fairfields had become displaced persons. The Ireland of their father's youth was the promised land never to be regained, especially for Winnie and Cissie. Lettie got to know the real Ireland, and had friends there in political circles. Cissie only went to Ireland once in her life, and not until she was seventy-nine.

Charles Fairfield was actually born at 2 Day Street in Tralee—a small house, "pinched Georgian," as Cissie described it when, with Lettie, she finally searched for her father's roots. Charles and his brothers were brought up between Kerry and Dublin; in Kerry they also had a "shooting-lodge" at Mounteagle, north of Tralee in Stack's Mountains— which the girls all their lives rendered as "Stag Mountains," proof that their family history depended on word-of-mouth tradition. (When Cissie and Lettie tracked the shooting-lodge down in 1971 they found "a tiny cottage in a glade in a cleft of the moors, looking down on what had been a lawn surrounded by rhododendrons.") In 1853, when Charles was twelve, his father died, and all the property reverted to the family of Charles George's first wife. His second wife and her sons were homeless.

Arabella Rowan Fairfield was a devout woman, and after her husband's death she joined the Plymouth Brethren, a sect whose austerity further curtailed the family's possibilities. The story was that she declined to go on taking the royal annuity on discovering that it had its roots in immorality. Her chief source of income was rents from run-down prop-

was getting on badly with her mother anyway. Mrs. Fairfield was even more anxious than Winnie on seeing her youngest daughter becoming a *feministe enragée;* it is impossible to overstress the distaste and horror with which the militants were regarded by the majority of both men and women. Nor did Cissie get on with her headmistress, Miss Ainslie, who made few allowances for her home situation or her political commitment. There was some sort of trouble at school, and a spell of illness—a tubercular infection of the left lung. Cissie left school under a cloud, with no mention of further education. Sensible Lettie suggested that she look for office work.

9

Music was central to the Fairfields' life, but for Cissie it came second to the theatre. She had been thrilled, at ten, by Sarah Bernhardt in *La Dame aux Camélias,* and in her teen-age years she saw Mrs. Patrick Campbell, Ellen Terry, and the singer Yvette Guilbert. She found time, in addition to her suffragette activities, not only to see plays but also to act in them. Both plays and protest marches were in a sense public appearances, and perhaps complemented one another; theatre stories in her letters to Lettie come hard on the heels of her accounts of demonstrations. She saw nearly every production that came to Edinburgh, including the risqué *What Every Woman Knows* by J. M. Barrie.

She belonged to an amateur dramatic company run by Graeme Goring, for whom she had little respect. He was "a perfect and entire Ass, with an absorbing reverence for the romantic drama," though she acknowledged that he had something to teach her about "the voice." She despised the little-girl parts she was inevitably asked to play, and described to Lettie the "awful ordeal" of having to "enter the room dancing, my hands behind my back, singing."

When, at fifteen, she went backstage at the King's Theatre in Edinburgh while the Christmas pantomime was in production, she thought that both she and Flora Duncan were "better looking than the actresses," as she told Lettie. Cissie had fine dark hair, a wide forehead, a wide mouth, large bright dark eyes, and a well-developed if stocky figure that was to cause her problems later—"my sturdy pack-horse build," as she was to call it. Her own opinion was that although she was not a beauty she was "capable in certain conditions of reminding people of beauty," although "I have ugly feet and ankles, I have always known it."

She had both the appearance and the temperament to make a career on the stage, though there were counter-indications. One of these was, paradoxically, her tendency to react histrionically to crises in ordinary life. She was claustrophobic; she tended to express emotional strain by physical collapse; her high-strung nervousness also showed in a skin-irritation on her wrists and hands, and a slight involuntary facial grimace, both of which affected her under stress. Her "twitch," Winnie candidly said, was enough in itself to prevent her from being a success on the stage. Cissie's sisters, though they marvelled at her exploits, refused to be impressed by her.

In April 1910, aged seventeen, she went to London to audition for the Academy of Dramatic Art in Gower Street, which had been founded only six years before. (Later it became the Royal Academy of Dramatic Art, known as RADA.) "I fainted in the Tube going up, at Baker Street. . . . Three very nice women came and looked after me, and one asked, 'Are you going to meet anyone who'll look after you—a sister?' 'No', I muttered piteously, 'A theatrical manager', and closed my eyes. I then heard a whisper. 'Poor child—an actress!'"

After this fine performance, she was seen and heard at the Academy by the administrator, Kenneth Barnes, and three others. "Oh, the 'manner'! They all sat and looked 'brilliant'. They were kind, though." She was accepted, to begin at the end of the month. She collapsed again afterwards on the doorstep of a friend of Lettie's in York Road, Lambeth, and, the friend being out, was succoured by her room-mate, Chris Hartley.

Chris Hartley, older than Cissie, shortly married and became Chris Bishop; she was to be a close friend. It was with Chris that Cissie went to the first London performance of Chekhov's The Cherry Orchard, when the audience, after howling with derision during the first act, ended up applauding wildly. The Bishops belonged to the Fabian Society, and it was on that initial meeting in York Road that Cissie first heard scandal about the famous author and former Fabian H. G. Wells.

Chris told Cissie, and Cissie reported to Lettie, that in his novel *Ann Veronica* "Wells has given every particular of the proceedings c.f. Amber Reeves, after she became insane from over-study." What Wells, a twice-married man in his forties, had actually depicted in his novel was his passionately sexual affair with young Amber, the daughter of his friends and fellow-Fabians Maud and Pember Reeves. This had been published six months before; the current scandal was in fact the recent birth of Amber's daughter by Wells. Obviously, Cissie had not yet read *Ann Veronica*; and her new friend had censored the gossip for the young girl's ears.

10

Cissie's Edinburgh life was over. Like both her sisters, she left the scene of her eventful girlhood without a tear. She rarely talked about Edinburgh, and rarely wrote about "the Scottish blight that ruined my early life." It was connected with fatherlessness, with being poor and socially uneasy. Her mother's bitterness against her husband had infected those years, and fuelled Cissie's ecstatic feminism. In her Edinburgh-set novel, *The Judge,* the young heroine remembers "no good of her father," who is depicted as an emptily boastful Irishman, "a specialist in disappointment."

The Fairfield household moved back to London. Winnie had qualified as a teacher, and took a post in a boys' preparatory school. Lettie was employed by the London County Council as medical officer for schools. They found a small semi-detached house in Chatham Close in the Hampstead Garden Suburb, on the extreme northern edge of the capital. It was a brand-new development of cheap, cottage-style housing; there was a long way to walk to shops or public transport to the city centre, but it was quiet. They called the house Fairliehope, after a farmhouse with a view over the Forth they had liked in the Pentland Hills.

The new house was not far from where Aunt Sophie and Uncle Arthur Fairfield lived in Golders Green. Before her mother moved south, Cissie had to stay with Aunt Sophie, and hated it. Both Cissie and Winnie believed that Aunt Sophie was a morphine addict. This forceful woman approved of Lettie, who was hardworking, responsible, and successful, and disapproved of headstrong Cissie, who in turn resented her bitterly.

Cissie tended to externalize her problems, attributing failure or unhappiness to a malign fate. One of the last friends in her long life was the comedian Frankie Howerd. In the car after a lunch with him in the 1970s, she asked him whether he felt that the fates were against him—clearly expecting the answer "Yes." When he replied that he felt that anything that had gone wrong was generally a result of his own mistakes, she was silent. It was not just fate that Cissie blamed for her own troubles but, very often, a particular person, the intimate enemy. Aunt Sophie had been generous during the difficult years, but for Cissie, whose fragile self-esteem she had damaged, she became the prototype of a series of monsters in human form. "The darkness and fear of my childhood was due to one person; who became several."

Cissie attended the Academy of Dramatic Art for three terms (the full course was four), from April 1910 to the end of March 1911, at 12 guineas a term. By her own account, she did not do well there. She had come with a recommendation from the actress Rosina Filippi, who had heard her recite in Edinburgh. Miss Filippi had taught at the Academy, but left before Cissie arrived; Cissie ascribed her own lack of success to the fact that Filippi and the administrator, Kenneth Barnes, had parted on bad terms. She was also self-conscious about her "twitch," and felt at a disadvantage because she could not afford good clothes. The greatest friend she made there, Greta Wood, recalled three-quarters of a century later how half Cissie's false moustache fell off while she was playing Antonio in *The Merchant of Venice*, humiliating her in front of Mr. Barnes, who was not kind.

But Cissie, always articulate and outspoken, learned at the Academy how to control and project her voice. Though she still had the light voice of a young girl, it became resonant and expressive, any Edinburgh intonation—"that delightful pinched Edinburgh accent"—eradicated. She left the Academy "beaten," as she felt, but determined, at eighteen years of age, to find work in the theatre for herself. She got the part of Regina in a production of Ibsen's *Ghosts,* and a small part in *Phyl,* a play by Cicely Hamilton which was performed in Eastbourne and in the theatre on Brighton's West Pier during the summer season.

She became a writer "without choosing to do so—at home we all wrote and thought nothing of it." She was still at the Academy when her first journalism was published: a review of Gorky's play *The Lower Depths,* for the London *Evening Standard.* The regular theatre critic was unable to go, and gave her the two free tickets (she took Lettie with her) on condition that she send in a notice. After this successful coup she called on the London bureau chief of the Melbourne *Argus*—the same man who had employed her father—and asked him for work. He told her to "find something more suitable to do than writing," and proceeded to give a job to the child of another former colleague, who happened to be a boy. But Cissie found a better platform.

The first issue of *The Freewoman,* a feminist weekly, appeared on 23 November 1911. The editor and leader-writer was a young woman from Lancashire, Dora Marsden, whom Cissie thought "one of the most beautiful women I have ever seen." She was a close friend of Mary Gawthorpe, Cissie's patron and heroine, who at this stage was co-editor though she soon fell out with Dora Marsden over the latter's critical attitude to the WSPU. In the second issue of *The Freewoman,* on 30 November, there was a review of a book about the position of women in Indian life; the reviewer was Cicily (*sic*) Fairfield, and she began her piece with a bang: "There are two kinds of imperialists—imperialists and bloody imperialists." (Shaw's *Pygmalion,* in which the phrase "Not bloody likely" elicited gasps of scandalized laughter from the audience, was not performed until 1913.) She liked to go for the jugular in her first sentence, as in a review of Strindberg's published plays: "Writers on the subject of August Strindberg have hitherto omitted to mention that he could not write."

It was the following spring when Cissie began using a pseudonym, chiefly in order to pacify her anxious mother. Much could be made of her choice of the name "Rebecca West," a character in Ibsen's play *Rosmersholm* who is the mistress of a married man and compels him to join

her in a melodramatic double suicide by drowning. Cissie Fairfield was
no one's mistress, and she came to regret the Ibsen connection, insisting
that she chose the name in a hurry when the paper was going to press,
and that she liked neither the play nor the character. It was Ibsen, she
wrote in middle life, who first taught her that it was ideas that make the
world go round, but soon "I began to realize that Ibsen cried out for ideas
for the same reason that men call out for water, because he had not
got any."

But no one would choose to sail under a flag that she actively repu-
diated, and, indeed, Ibsen's Rebecca West speaks some lines which (as
her friend the columnist Bernard Levin said at her memorial service in
1983) might have been written to sum up her flesh-and-blood namesake:
"Live, work, act. Don't sit here and brood and grope among insoluble
enigmas." Many of those unfamiliar with Ibsen's work, and who only
knew this marvellous girl as Rebecca West, assumed from the name that
she was Jewish. She was in fact, both by temperament and circum-
stances, an honorary Jew. The Hampstead Garden Suburb and the ad-
jacent suburb of Hendon were favoured by members of the Jewish
community who were less impoverished than those in the East End of
London but less prosperous than those who lived in Hampstead or in
Golders Green. Many of Rebecca's closest friends, from girlhood on, were
Jewish.

Hers was an instantly successful pseudonym. She was transformed
into Rebecca West not only in professional but in personal life as well, at
least with new friends. To her family, she remained Cissie.

11

Rebecca met new people at *The Freewoman's* fort-
nightly discussion circle, where she was a lively presence—it was too
much like being in church, she thought—always seeking to open feminist questions out to include literature and philosophy. In May 1912 she

read an ambitious paper to the circle on "Interpretations of Life," about duality between man and woman and between God and man.

God existed, then and later, for Rebecca. Her quarrel with Him as a girl was that He did not take the responsibility for crimes committed in His name. A "new God" would grow out of man's humanity to man—that is, out of socialism: "If we see that life is ordered so that humanity may flower unstinted by poverty and unhappiness . . . a God will come to us born of the human will." Her socialist feminism found fault with the established church, which panicked "if women show any signs of having close relations with Christ."

Lettie had joined the Fabian Women's Group as soon as the Fairfields moved to London, and as a woman doctor was particularly welcomed. Her younger sisters joined the Fabians in her wake, and Rebecca, still in her teens, met luminaries such as George Bernard Shaw, a frequent speaker. She admired his "greyhound" appearance, his athletic bearing, his voice, and his eloquence. "The effect he created was more stupendous since in those days every well-to-do man wore stuffy clothes, ate too much, took too little exercise, and consequently looked like a bolster." But she did not, in her maturer years, admire his work: "I passionately resent the fact that God gave him a beautiful style and that he used it to preach tedious and reactionary ideas." Nor did she continue to admire him as a male specimen: on account of his sexless marriage, he became "a eunuch perpetually inflamed by flirtation."

In September 1912 Rebecca West wrote two articles which had important consequences. One was a notice of *The New Humpty-Dumpty* by Ford Madox Hueffer, until recently editor of *The English Review,* in which her piece appeared. Hueffer had published the book under a pseudonym; Rebecca's humorous notice made the book's true authorship clear to anyone who could read between the lines, and Hueffer asked her to tea.

Or, rather, Violet Hunt did. She and Hueffer were living in London as man and wife at her house, South Lodge, 80 Campden Hill Road. Violet Hunt was a novelist with private means, well past her first youth, who had had many lovers (including H. G. Wells). She and Hueffer entertained young literary people—"*les Jeunes,*" as they called their protégés—and Rebecca became part of the group. Violet Hunt recorded her first impression of an ingenue Rebecca, in a pink frock and a "country-girlish" straw hat that hid her "splendid liquid eyes." She sat with her feet planted firmly together, her satchel-like handbag in her lap; she was "the ineffable schoolgirl," with a voice like milk and honey. She was "quite superiorly, ostentatiously young"—yet, said Violet Hunt, she already had Fleet Street at her feet. Her articles and reviews were making "not so much a splash, as a hole in the world." Rebecca West, in short, was news.

In *The English Review,* from which he had recently been dislodged, Hueffer had published new work by Thomas Hardy, Henry James, H. G. Wells, D. H. Lawrence, and Ezra Pound; Rebecca in retrospect thought it "the most impressive periodical ever to appear in our language." She found Hueffer wanting as a man—"stout, gangling, albino-ish"—and told G. B. Stern, the ebullient young Jewish woman novelist whom she met at South Lodge and who became her best friend, that being embraced by him was like being the toast under a poached egg. Yet she admired him not only as an editor but also as a writer, hailing what was to be his best-known novel, *The Good Soldier,* when it appeared in 1915 as "a much, much better book than any of us deserve." (By this time, on account of the war with Germany, he had changed his name to Ford Madox Ford.)

Violet Hunt was a poor man's Lady Ottoline Morrell both in her appearance and her way of life. In her drawing-room, decorated with William Morris wallpaper and chintzes, she gave the tea parties where, in the ensuing months, Rebecca was to meet, among others, the writers Compton Mackenzie, Somerset Maugham, and May Sinclair.

It was Wyndham Lewis, another South Lodge regular (he painted a red abstract panel to hang over Hueffer's study mantelpiece), who was the first to publish Rebecca West's fiction—a lurid story of sexual antagonism entitled "Indissoluble Matrimony," begun when she was still an aspiring actress and turned down by both *The English Review* and *The Blue Review.* Lewis printed it in the first issue of *Blast* in 1914. Much later, in 1932, he did a drawing of her, which she kept until she died."*

Brigit Patmore, one of the young women guests of whom Hueffer was particularly fond, described Rebecca at the South Lodge parties making "incredibly hair-raising and wicked" observations in her soft, musical voice. A lot of the conversation was radical and feminist: Violet Hunt was a suffragist and wrote for *The Freewoman*—which came to an abrupt end

* Now in the National Portrait Gallery, London.

ounces of Lady Betty wool for socks for Anthony." She loved the child, but "I want to live an unfettered and adventurous life like a Bashibazouk, and spend all my money on buying clothes in Bond Street." In Anthony, she said, she was "laying up treasure for the hereafter (i.e., dinners at the Carlton* in 1936) but what I want now is ROMANCE. Something with a white face and a slight natural wave in the dark hair and a large grey touring-car is what I really need." H. G. Wells did not fit this description; but she loved him too, more than she admitted to Sylvia Lynd.

At the Lynds' house in Hampstead, Rebecca made a new friend, the historian Philip Guedalla. In her social life as in her professional life, she was not wholly dependent on her lover. She picked up her political interests, attending the Fabian Summer Schools in the Lake District; Shaw, now over sixty, teased the actress Mrs. Patrick Campbell by telling her how he had struck up a "precipitous flirtation" there with Rebecca, who could "handle a pen as brilliantly as I ever could, and much more savagely. We fell into each other's arms intellectually and artistically." Rebecca gave a lecture on feminism, and rowed on the lake with other elderly Fabians.

She had been taken on by Wells's literary agent, J. B. Pinker, and in 1916 her *Henry James* was published. It sold only six hundred copies, but caused comment: the literary establishment found it offensive that a twenty-three-year-old should feel free to criticize the Master, particularly since he had been dead only a few months. Her short book still stands as a fair introduction to the man and his work. She faults James for his lack of intellectual passion, asking why "books about ideas" are generally so bad since "the genius of M. Anatole France and Mr Wells have proved that they need not be so"; it must be, she said, that most people "reserve passion for their personal relationships and therefore never 'feel' an idea with the sensitive fingertips of affection." She was funny about James's idea of women, and about the Jamesian sentence, "a delicate creature swathed in relative clauses as an invalid in shawls." Her criticism was more levelheaded than that of her mentor Ford Madox Ford, whose hagiographical *Henry James* had appeared four years before; her astringency was contained within a context that acknowledged the "white light" of James's genius.

* The Carlton Grill, a restaurant—not the Carlton Club, a Conservative stronghold.

H. G. Wells had an ambivalent friendship with Henry James—their aims and techniques as novelists could hardly have been more opposed—and while Rebecca was writing her book he had been making cruel fun of the Jamesian manner in *Boon* (also published in 1916). He defended Rebecca's book, writing to the novelist Hugh Walpole that "my blood still boils at the thought of those pretentious academic greasers conspiring to put down a friendless girl (who can write any of them out of sight) in the name of loyalty to literature."

Rebecca West, successful and attractive, might not seem a "friendless girl" but, as Wells understood, it was how she saw herself. As an unmarried mother she was someone who many "nice people" would not want to know. Socialists and Fabians tended to be puritan; it was not among them that Rebecca was to find unquestioning acceptance, but among more worldly people such as St. Loe Strachey of the *Spectator* and his wife, Amy, and the society hostess Lady Colefax. One of her chief champions was the thriller-writer Marie Belloc-Lowndes, the confidante of fashionable London (Wells described her as "the most attractive tea-cosy I have ever met"), who praised Rebecca's diffidence, touched by seeing her blush "when I once told her that I regarded her short study of Henry James as one of the best critical works in the language."

It was with Mrs. Belloc-Lowndes that Rebecca met the man to whom Wells had defended her, Hugh Walpole. "Because he is a triffic [*sic*] celebrity he sat still while Miss Stern and I handed round tea and cakes to the old ladies." She had offended the "triffic celebrity" shortly before, by an acid review. He had written her a petulant letter, to which she replied that she did not conceal her feelings when she thought people were writing nonsense, nor when she thought they were writing "sensibly and beautifully"; "if people choose to remember the far less frequent occasions of my dislike rather than the quite numerous occasions of my appreciation it is hardly my fault!" Professionally, she was forceful. Privately, she was the friendless girl.

When as an elderly woman she read the account of her youthful modesty in Mrs. Belloc-Lowndes's published letters and diaries, she wrote in her own diary that she had loved Mrs. Belloc-Lowndes. "I think she must have loved me a little. How dignified she was. I am not gentle and I have had my dignity cut away from me, *sawn off,* by all the people I have ever had anything to do with. . . . It was my loneliness. I had no one to back me."

Rebecca West was never complacent or conceited. As an old and famous woman she rarely referred to her own work, except when interviewers obliged her to do so, and then only to confess her difficulties. Those who found her imperious could not possibly know that she saw herself as an underdog. She fought her own corner, and she championed the cause of fellow-underdogs. "Were it possible for us to wait for ourselves to come into the room, not many of us would find our hearts breaking into flower as we heard the door-handle turn. But we fight for our rights, we will not let anybody take our breath away from us, and we resist all attempts to prevent us from using our wills."

5

In the year of her *Henry James*, Wells spent the late summer touring the French and Italian war fronts for a book. From abroad, he spelled out to Rebecca how their lives might be improved. "I wish we could fix up some sort of life that would detach us lovers a little more from the nursery." The way things were, "it's really a very severe test of my love for you." Above all, "Clear Wilma out. This is an ultimatum."

They made a new arrangement. Wells took rooms in a boarding-house at 51 Claverton Street, in the Pimlico district of London, where he and Rebecca could be together alone. In the spring of 1917 she and Anthony moved to a modest modern house on Marine Parade at Leigh-on-Sea on the Essex coast. The house was called Southcliffe; it was semi-detached, and covered in decorative woodwork. Marine Parade, on a cliff above the wide estuary of the Thames, commanded a magnificent view. G. B. Stern—Gladys, usually called "Peter," though Rebecca called her "Tynx"—took Wilma Meikle's place, and spent much of her time with

Rebecca, who was happier at Southcliffe, "a jolly little house" and the first home that she had liked.

Anthony could play down on the beach, where winkle-sellers had their huts. The railway at Leigh runs behind the beach, at the foot of the cliff on which Marine Parade is built; from her house Rebecca only had to walk down the steep grassy slope and cross a metal bridge to reach the station and the train to London. At Leigh, Anthony, seeing the red sun go down, said to his mother, "Do it again!," as if her power commanded the sunsets.

He was three that year, and only now did Rebecca feel able to take him home to see her mother in the Hampstead Garden Suburb. Mrs. Fairfield's pleasure in the child mended the breach. "Mother simply adored him, and gave him every privilege a favourite little boy can have." Mrs. Fairfield's extant letters confirm this version of her feelings for "the little precious." Only when she was terminally ill did she decline to see him, not wanting the child to remember her as disfigured. (It is typical of the opposing versions of his childhood that Anthony claimed only to remember seeing his grandmother on her deathbed.) Rebecca began to go to church again, for the first time in five years. "Anthony whiled away the time with his collection of winkles. I had no such consolations," she wrote in her diary; but she kept on going to church.

Her life was restless; she rarely spent as much as a week in one place. In Leigh she worked, and spent time with Anthony; in London, from their base in Claverton Street, she and Wells dined out, went to theatres, film and music halls. They saw his friends, mostly literary and political—Arnold Bennett (who never liked Rebecca, nor she him), E. S. P. Haynes (who suddenly kissed her passionately, "amazing incident")—and hers, mostly literary and theatrical—Violet Hunt (now "raving mad"), William Archer, the translator of Ibsen and "a dear creature," the actress and writer Fryn Tennyson Jesse, the impresario Nigel Playfair, Sara Melville, the Lynds, her sisters.

Rebecca's favourite restaurant was Le Petit Riche, "such a nasty place now," according to Sylvia Lynd after she and her husband first dined there with Rebecca on an occasion when the other guests were E. S. P. Haynes and his wife. "It was a strange party, joined later by Wells and Bennett," Sylvia reported to her mother. "Bennett is a rather vulgar and provincial-voiced person and smoked the last piece of his cigar stuck on the end of a pen-knife. He had been dining with Wells at the Reform Club and had swallowed a good deal of champagne, so perhaps that accounted for his vulgarity."

Wells, Sylvia Lynd thought, had much better manners, "full of deliberate impudences of course in his talk but not gauche and intentionally boorish like Bennett. Also he does not cut his conversation according to his company. A good mark for H.G." But in spite of her liking and admiration for Rebecca, Sylvia was "rather horrified" that Wells had come at all. "My sense of propriety believes in neat compartments and it was a flooding of the bulkheads. . . . Besides I like Janie [Wells], and all the non-jealousy business is humbug—only done as the price of the Pasha's company—converting all their sounds of woe to Hey nonny nonny."

Rebecca, in private, could not always suppress her sounds of woe. Her divided life, as Mrs. Townshend had foreseen, was not suiting her. Stress manifested itself in nervous illnesses and skin-trouble; she sought relaxation with face-massages, and found solace in impulse-buying—extravagant "silk evening knickers" and other luxuries, from the best shops.

Wells optimistically expected her London life with him, her home life with Anthony, and her writing life to be carried out harmoniously. He had already, in *The Research Magnificent* (1915), depicted the Rebecca he had first loved as Amanda, "the freest, finest, bravest spirit" the hero had ever met. Panther and Jaguar were playfully transformed into Leopard and Cheetah. But Wells used the novel to send Rebecca warning messages. There are serious temperamental conflicts between the life-enhancing Amanda and her lover: she is over-dramatic, undisciplined, always ill, and insufficiently supportive of his high intellectual purposes and need for order.

In 1916 Wells published *Mr Britling Sees It Through*, a war novel from the home front. His heroine—"it seemed unreasonable that anyone shouldn't be in love with her"—is actually named Cissie, and has a sister named Letty. He used the Fairfields' private slang ("boof'l young man") and placed a baby in Cissie's arms: "She looked like a silvery Madonna." But the baby belongs to Letty, who, in the novel, is married.

The fictional Letty's husband in *Mr Britling* is lost, or maybe amnesiac; Rebecca West's first novel, *The Return of the Soldier*, turns entirely on the partial amnesia of a shell-shocked officer, and the healing significance of parenthood. Her humble heroine was modelled, she said, on

my life mainly to repair the carelessness of one moment. It has been no good and I am tired of it."

On the same day, Rebecca was writing to S. K. Ratcliffe about the "appalling life" she led with Wells, his "increasing nervous instability" and fits of "almost maniacal rage" alternating with "weeks of childish dependence." Wells was not in such a desperate mental state as this would suggest—he had offered himself (unsuccessfully) as a Labour parliamentary candidate, and in 1922–23 he published four books and countless articles—but it was how he presented himself to Rebecca, in protest and appeal.

But they still could not keep away from each other. A few weeks later they entertained Sinclair Lewis and his wife, Gracie, and all Wells's possessive jealousy returned—"the humiliation it was to see Sinclair Lewis slobber his way up your arm . . . My Panther." At the first international conference of PEN on 1 May, Rebecca and he sat together, both turning their heads defensively away from the recording camera. It was more like planning a divorce than the end of an affair, as was reflected in Wells's phrase "You may marry again," and in Rebecca's comment to S. K. Ratcliffe that, "as I have a steady monogamous nature and would have been the most wifely wife on earth," it was always hard not to give in to Wells and "take the job" again.

There were fatal differences between them about what each wanted from the other, and from life. There were fatal similarities as well. They had the same broad humour. Both were socially unplaced, both had had patchy educations. Wells complained about Rebecca's inconvenient illnesses, but "disabling physical collapses had been his stock response to stress" also; and in anger "he became infected with the paranoia that often affects the persecuted." His "tendency to overrespond to personal criticism which became part of his character in his late fifties" raised "the explosive outburst to the level of an art form." These characteristics, which Wells would have been the first to pin on Rebecca, were ascribed to him by their son, Anthony—a prejudiced witness in his father's favour, so his remarks need not be read as overstatements. Rebecca's chief complaints against Wells—"his indiscipline, his disorderliness, his refusal to face facts, his capacity for magnifying the smallest mischance into a major catastrophe"—always sound exactly like Wells's against Rebecca.

Why did they not break up earlier, and more easily? Wells was ageing, and may have doubted whether he would ever again find a young woman so sexually and intellectually exciting as Rebecca. Neither wanted to be the one who was left: each wanted to be the one who made the break. For Rebecca, Wells was her first and only lover, mentor, protector, enchanter. Being in his company, she recorded half a century later, was "on a level with seeing Nureyev dance or hearing Tito Gobbi sing." Anthony, and his need for two parents, was their joint concern and at the root of Rebecca's desire for marriage with Wells. Marriage is of use, wrote Rebecca in 1925, "for rivetting the fact of paternity in the male mind" (in an article with the feisty title "I Regard Marriage with Fear and Horror").

Rebecca in the 1920s was, as an American paper declared, "the personification of all the vitality, the courage and the independence of the modern woman," but her girlhood had been Edwardian and her parents had been Victorians. The word "mistress" aroused expectations which her life with Wells had not answered. "It is impudent of men to keep women as luxuries," she wrote nearly twenty years later, "unless they have the power to guarantee them the framework of luxury. . . . But if they fail to keep that ambitious promise, which there was indeed no obligation to make, they should surrender the system and let women go back to freedom and get what they can." Wells had failed her on both counts, and held on for his own convenience. "I ought to have liberated her," he acknowledged in old age. "I realize I got much the best out of our relationship."

12

When Wells and Rebecca were semi-separated in the spring of 1923, he (without her knowledge) became involved with a young Austrian journalist, Hedwig Verena Gatternigg, who had first approached him on professional matters. She declared herself to be passionately in love with him. He, flattered, and smarting from Rebecca's apparent flirtation with Sinclair Lewis, succumbed on numerous occasions, but then determined to put an end to the tiresome affair.

The distraught Gatternigg, naked under her mackintosh, turned up at his flat at Whitehall Court as he was dressing to go out to dinner with Edwin Montagu, Secretary of State for India, and was shown into the study. According to his own, much later account, Wells called for the hall porter to have her shown out, whereupon she cut herself across the wrists and armpits with a razor. The hall porter and two policemen had the bleeding but still-voluble girl removed to hospital. There was every danger of the story's getting into the press; reporters were soon pestering both him and Rebecca in the hope of a major scandal.

Wells had given Gatternigg a letter of introduction to Rebecca, presumably to deflect her attention from himself, and the girl had called on her before the visit to Whitehall Court. Rebecca had found her manifestly neurotic, and was quite prepared to help H.G. out in this crisis. "I remember sitting with her in Kensington Gardens," Wells wrote, "on the morning after the scene in my flat. . . . So often we had attacked each other with unjust interpretations and unreasonable recriminations that it matters very much to my memories that we sat and talked and were very sane and wise." Rebecca agreed to speak to those newspaper proprietors whom she knew personally, and ask them not to carry the story. (This was only partly successful.) She and Wells closed ranks conspicuously, lunching together at the Ivy after their talk and attending a first night that evening. Wells felt that the incident had drawn them closer together. In fact, it only hardened her resolve to detach herself from him.

The Gatternigg affair boomeranged half a century later, causing Rebecca fresh pain and humiliation. She told Wells's official biographers and Gordon Ray, author of H. G. Wells and Rebecca West, that Wells had only a brief and trivial involvement with the Austrian girl, and that it had been Jane Wells who discovered her in the flat and telephoned for the police. Those who knew better—notably Gip Wells, H.G.'s elder son—contradicted this story when it appeared in print; Rebecca was assumed to have falsified her account. Jane Wells was at home in the country on 20 June; the previous night, she had given a party at Easton to celebrate Gip's graduation.

Rebecca believed her account was true because it was what Wells had told her when they were being "sane and wise" in Kensington Gardens. It was Gordon Ray's manuscript that revealed to her the true nature and duration of Wells's relationship with Gatternigg; she was specially upset to learn that he had spent a whole weekend with the girl. She wrote out her unhappiness in her diary, and in her private notebook tried to take in the other lie he had told her: "It was not Jane who discovered the body [sic], though H.G. told me that she did, it was H.G." His lies were a sad time-bomb, exploding in the 1970s, when she was old.

After the Gatternigg affair, Rebecca went to Marienbad ("a mixture between Hell and Bournemouth") with two women friends, to take the cure. Wells turned up, by arrangement, on his way to see President Masaryk of Czechoslovakia, and, disturbed himself, disturbed her peace of mind. "You were happy at Marienbad before I came and spoilt it." On her return, Rebecca confessed to Sara Melville that she had agreed to go back to him. If she did, she told Mrs. Melville, he would give her £20,000 for Anthony: "I don't gamble on making that myself because I feel dead beat." She could, she said (quite untruthfully), "have made H.G. get divorced and marry me, he wanted so much to get me back, but I thought it wiser not to."

Letters about this latest development whizzed between Lettie and G. B. Stern, who regretted that money should have been a deciding factor "when it was a question of her own personal health and happiness." But since marriage was out of the question, money for Anthony was Rebecca's considered priority. Going back to Wells in order to secure it was part of a strategy. "After all," she wrote to Sylvia Lynd, "the way I stuck to Wells for Anthony's sake . . . gives me, I think, the right not to be considered hysterical and impulsive in these matters."

Having secured support for Anthony, Rebecca was staking all on her escape to America. She, Wells, and Anthony had a last holiday in the summer of 1923 in Swanage, from where she warned her agent that "there will be no book this autumn"; but she had just received from him £875.9.0 in royalties on her two novels. Anthony went back to school at St. Piran's in September. In October, Rebecca left on the *Mauretania* for the United States. As Wells conceded, "the effective break came from her."

His letters followed her. He was more hurt to lose her, he acknowledged later, than she was to be quit of him. "Bored. Wants his Black Pussy. His *dear* Black Pussy. His soft kind Pussy—all others being shams and mutations. Wants to know when she is coming back to him." There was something else that Wells did not know. Rebecca, who had never been unfaithful to him, was interested in another man—an interest that was to become an obsession.

PART THREE

Sunflower